"The offspring of an improbable liaison between Surrealism and the American vernacular, these poems will get under your skin. This is poetry as discovery, and what John Leax found implicit in the tabloid headlines is rich and strange indeed."
—John Wilson, Editor, *Books & Culture*

"In *Tabloid News* John Leax probes the mythic underbelly of the American unconscious with hilariously unsettling results. By applying method to the madness, Leax shows us the tragicomedy lying within 'fear and desire.' These poems are fun-house mirrors, reflecting back to us both our need for and our dread of the Other. And yet they also demonstrate a yearning for metamorphosis, for an ultimate union in which beauty and ugliness are made one by grace."
—Gregory Wolfe, Editor, *Image* journal

Tabloid News

Tabloid News

poems by
John Leax

WORDFARM
LA PORTE, INDIANA

Also by John Leax

Reaching into Silence (1974)

In Season and Out (1985)

The Task of Adam (1985)

Nightwatch (1989)

Country Labors (1991)

Standing Ground (1991)

Grace Is Where I Live (1993, 2004)

Out Walking (2000)

WordFarm
2010 Michigan Avenue
La Porte, IN 46350
www.wordfarm.net
info@wordfarm.net

Cover Images: Veer, iStockphoto

Design: Andrew Craft

USA ISBN 0-9743427-6-9
Printed in the United States of America
First WordFarm Edition: 2005

Library of Congress Cataloging-in-Publication Data

Leax, John.
  Tabloid news : poems / John Leax.-- 1st WordFarm ed.
    p. cm.
  ISBN-13: 978-0-9743427-6-4
  ISBN-10: 0-9743427-6-9 (pbk.)
  1. Newspapers--Headlines--Poetry. 2. Tabloid newspapers--Poetry. 3. Current events--Poetry. I. Title.
  PS3562.E262T25 2005
  811'.54--dc22

                                                                    2005005942

P 10 9 8 7 6 5 4 3 2 1
Y 12 11 10 09 08 07 06 05

Acknowledgments

Books & Culture: "Meet the Amazing Half Man Half Pig," "Montana Police Shoot Bigfoot" and "I Want to Have a Space Alien's Baby"

The Chaffin Journal: "Bizarre Creature Spotted in Louisiana Bayou"

Image: "Adoption Agency Sells Shaven Apes as Human Infants" and "Duck Hunters Shoot Angel"

The New Pantagruel: "Baby Born with Antlers," "Smartest Ape in the World Goes to College" and "Real Life Cat Woman Found in the Ozarks and She's Looking for Love"

River King Poetry Supplement: "World's Fattest Twins Arrested for Stealing World's Fattest Cat"

For James Calvin Schaap

Contents

Preface: Writing
Tabloid News

In the fall of 2001, a month or so after the destruction of the World Trade Center, a tabloid headline caught my attention as I stood in the checkout line of my local grocery store: "Leaping Turtles Invade US." With the usual mixture of amusement and wonder the tabloids stir in me, I looked more closely. Then the accompanying image registered. Large snapping turtles had clamped onto the breasts of a group of women gathered at a pool and were pulling them to the ground.

The evening before, I had been reading the poems of Pattiann Rogers. I delight in her inclination in poems such as "Suppose Your Father Was a Redbird" to suggest an oddity and then explore it. It shouldn't have surprised me, but it did; right there at the register her poems and the image before me came together. Two lines sprang into my imagination, *Suppose one could believe the tabloid headlines. Suppose the stories under them were true.* I went home, went to my desk, and allowed them to play out into a poem apart from any logical or decorous censor. When I had exhausted the impulse, I had before me an oddball thing I assumed I would neither publish nor repeat.

The following spring, yielding to a whim and a need for comedy, I tacked it onto the end of a reading I gave at the

Calvin College Festival of Faith and Writing. Afterwards, a friend said to me, "So, you've written your 9/11 poem." I was stunned, for I had not associated the attack of the turtles with the attack on the Twin Towers. But my friend was right. The horror of that September morning had emerged unbidden in the dark comedy of my poem—so also had my fears and uncertainty about our militant responses.

I went out from the reading reevaluating my poem and wondering if the creator of the tabloid story might not have been deliberately touching something buried in the consciousness of the paper's readers. A few weeks later, when another headline, "Baby Born with Antlers," caught my eye, I realized that a deep desire for connection to things other than ourselves lay beneath the outlandishness of the headlines. Nothing else I could imagine could explain the regular presentation of the half-human half-animal monsters in the tabloid features. Then I recalled the late nineteenth-century fascination with Darwinian "missing links" that led to the carnival displays of freaks and the horrendous racism of the sideshows. That fascination also lived in the tabloids. Desire and fear. The inseparable linkage of the two explains the tabloid imagination.

I decided to follow the headlines and interrogate them. I would ask of each, "What desire, what fear is represented here?" And as I found answers, I would make poems. I set myself rules: I would not buy the tabloids. I would work only with the attraction of the headline and the image. I would make up my own stories, and I would respond only to headlines that joined humans with animals or some "other" such as a space alien or an angel.[1]

Over the next two-and-a-half years I would find a

surprising poignancy in the tabloids, a constant longing for transcendence and an equally constant though tragic fear of the animal body. Curiously, though the tabloids disappeared from the racks, in all that time I never saw one purchased. I never put a face with the longing or the fear that moved me as I wrote.

John Leax
Fillmore, New York
December 10, 2004

---

[1] *I violated my rules only once. A month or so after I wrote "Duck Hunters Shoot Angel," a follow-up headline, "Angel Forgives Duck Hunter," appeared. I couldn't resist opening the tabloid to learn the rest of the story. Across from that story I found the tale of the young woman who loved the space alien.*

Suppose one could believe the tabloid headlines.
Suppose the stories under them were true.

Leaping Turtles Invade US

Suppose a leaping turtle launching himself
four feet into the sultry air to fasten
his hooked beak in a woman's breast
and dangle as tenderly as a jewel.
Or suppose, lacking sufficient spring to reach
the breast, the turtle settling
for the vulnerable lower groin of an unsuspecting male.

Suppose one million turtles
possessing the reported temperament of killer bees
were heading north from a Mexican mountain camp.
Would you go out? Would you risk with your lover
a pondside stroll or a tryst beneath the shade
of a willow overhanging a sluggish stream?

You know you wouldn't.

You'd arm yourself against the terror
with a heavy-bladed kitchen knife
or a monumental cudgel or a pilfered .45.
Your first thought would be the thought of war
and your second would be of soup.

Suppose, this once, the headline has it right—
except for a small confusion about the leaping beast
that seizes the nurturing fount,

the engendering source.
Suppose that beast is you.

Could you doubt that turtles, outraged,
might adapt, give natural selection—their place
in the present scheme of things—the old heave-ho,
build their bodies and master martial arts?
Could you doubt that, shaped and disciplined
by persistence and age, they would emerge,
shells trimmed to a minimum weight,
muscles toned to steel by four thousand leg lifts
and as many painful squats, prepared to leap?

Suppose that leaping turtles are the active voice
of nature's long endurance.
Forget war. Forget soup. Think truce.

Baby Born with Antlers

Might we assume that he is a he?
Perhaps not. The antlered whitetail
familiar to our autumn woods
is a buck, but the reindeer doe
is antlered into spring.
There is no absolute in nature
on which to ground our thought.

We may, however, assume the mother bore
her child in pain. Look at those things!
Eight points, a rack for Boone and Crockett.
Let's hope the antlers were soft
and malleable, floating like golden locks
during the passage down the dark canal,
only hardening at the shock of air.
Or perhaps the birth was breech.
Either way, we may assume the child
cried at the slap of birth. There's nothing
new in that, nothing to report. But did
the mother cry? What did she think
when the midwife placed the child,
wet and wriggling, in her arms?
Did she scream, blurt out, "Monster!"
and push the double-natured thing away?

I think not. I think she recognized

her image in its flesh and loved him,
though she'd no warning of how,
when she nursed, she'd have to guard
her eyes from the sudden lifting
of his head. I think, when she first
held him, tenderly exploring his small
body, her hand touched a tiny hoof—
a baby born with antlers
would have, at least, two hooves—
and she thought, almost absently,
that she would purchase him a flute.

Adoption Agency Sells Shaven Apes as Human Infants

It could not last long, the sweet innocence
of the slightly flattened face,
the pink cuddliness of the body,
razor nicked and dimpled.
Nor could the simian strength, the quick
dexterity of the fingers,
or the precocious mobility be hidden.

Too quickly the ape-child would grow.
Tucked into bed, it would not cry.
It would take, instead, the bright mobile
suspended to stimulate its eyes
in its hand and swing easily from
the crib's confinement, drop to the floor,
break doors and locks to reach the warmth
of its mother's body, and climb
to ring its arms about her neck.

What would her observing husband think
as she moved about the house, their
dearly bought darling growing darkly
hirsute at two months, grinning
from her shoulder, smacking its lips
anticipating pleasure?

Would he be charmed or terrified?

Would he, looking into the eyes
of his wife, find tears, a fear matching
his own that something was awfully wrong?
Or would neither see, their need
to love—greater than any disappointment—
make the ape-child beautiful,
speak to its nature and give it a soul?
Would they in the fullness of time
take it to a priest for baptism?

And if they did, would you, a congregant,
rise up like an unwanted guest
at a wedding to announce a reason
why ape and child cannot be joined?
Or would you sit quietly,
watch the priest pour water
over the head so that it splashed
into the font of every blessing?
And if it splashed, a sparkling droplet
landing like spittle on your eye,
might you be changed, blessed?
Like the mother? Like the father?

Smartest Ape in the World Goes to College

Knowing the admissions department was by law
committed to a policy of nondiscrimination,
he applied. His test scores were excellent
and no campus visit was required. In reply
to the question, "What do you expect to gain
from a liberal arts education?" he wrote,
"It is my goal to become fully human."
His ambition led, of course, to admission
into an honors section. Orientation caused him fear—
he wasn't sure how to dress, and housing
worried him—he couldn't decide if coed
or single-sex was best. He went with coed,
figuring life in the presence of women
might be uplifting. Online
registration allowed him to avoid
actually meeting with his advisor,
though he felt the exchange of emails
valuable and enlightening. Concerned that
classmates and professors might find
his vocalizations awkward, he chose
large lectures over the intimacy
of smaller classes. But he could not
hide. He moved with an animal grace
that attracted women. His speech,
slow and often withheld, also worked
against him, his reticence projecting

a deep vulnerability and awakening
needs he meant to rise above.
He received many invitations. Shyly
he made excuses. He invented a girl
at home and retreated to his books.
He studied hard, played no sports,
and told no tales of conquest or
betrayal. Men thought him a bore.

For many months he was happy,
undisturbed in his belief
he could, by thought, add cubits
to his stature. He read Thoreau:
I know of no more encouraging
fact than the unquestioned ability
of man to elevate his life
by a conscious endeavor.

Then a darker, upstart poet
troubled his upward dream
of mobility. Descent with
modification suggested all
was chance. To be human marked no
final elevation, no end
achieved. Still the inward cry
of aspiration kept his soul

in motion. If Thoreau had found
within himself a half-starved hound,
a pilgrim saint, and learned
to reverence both, he too could be
a husband of the wild and walk
at peace in the sun-bright
wilderness of his division.

One day in Spring, invited
by a sprightly girl to picnic
in the college woods,
he took his chance in hand.
Beneath the trees, they touched
a wisdom not at all provincial.
The baying of a hound once lost
was heard as far as town. The saint
inscribed a poem in the bark.

World's Fattest Twins Arrested for Stealing World's Fattest Cat

Reportedly each weighs a ton and a half.
Seated side by side, brother and sister,
they are two slumping mountains,
the kind you find in coal country,
giving in to gravity, tailings at their feet.
Nothing about them is stable.

The twin on the right is called
Bald Mountain, for he has shaved his pate.
He is full of donuts and laughter.
The twin on the left is called
Black Forest, for she is hairy,
full of cake and melancholy.
Both are stay-at-homes.
They sit like comic monks and ruminate
on their hand-to-mouth existence.

Bald Mountain reads Nero Wolfe
and dreams of tending orchids
in a glass house. In his mind
the world is rational. In his heart
the world is Krispy Kreme.

Black Forest broods before a window
open to the street. She would like
to be in love, but the only man she knows

is her brother. She keeps a journal,
writing down what she sees—daffodils
in spring, mums in fall. Someday,
she hopes, Bald Mountain will read it
and be pleased—perhaps write her a poem.

It is Black Forest, at her window,
who sees the cat overflowing
the jogging stroller being rushed
down the street, taking all
the exercise it desires
breathing in and breathing out.

Black Forest is stunned by the weight
of glory. Her stomach rumbles.
She cuts a wedge of cake, stuffs it
in her mouth and chews.
It is not what she wants. Mumbling,
she points. Bald Mountain laughs
at the crumbs tumbling like a landslide
down the sunlit slopes of her breasts.

Then he too sees the cat—
resplendent, a long scarf flying
from the folds of its orange-striped neck,
a yowl of perfect delight

trailing in the wake of its coming.

That its cry signifies nothing
more than the promise of tuna
means nothing to Black Forest,
means nothing to Bald Mountain.
Vision has awakened in them longing,
and longing has stirred faith,
faith to move mountains.
As one they rise, push out the window,
and avalanche across the yard.
Neither grass nor shrub nor tree
can slow the crush of their desire.
All fall before them.

They snatch the cat—its owner
screaming for help, retreating,
terrified before their rude descent.
They clutch it to themselves,
name it Beyond Desire.

It snarls, turns ugly and scratches.
Black Forest hides her face.
Bald Mountain lets loose and weeps.
A siren calls in the distance.
The mountains do not move.

Dog Makes $60 Million Modeling

He found the dog in Batavia. Reluctantly
west of the Hudson for the first time
since he'd left home for instant glam,
he had time to kill. He roamed a small-town
mall, walked dumbly past Spencer's Gifts,
Fashion Bug, and Styles for the Big and Tall.
He sipped a Subway coffee and made up quips
for later use at bright-light parties,
for city laughs. At the mall end, a runway
cobbled together from folding tables
wrapped in purple crepe paper and dotted
with yellow tissue carnations stopped him.

Eight girls in empire gowns provided
by Leslie's New and Used Bridal Shop
were arranged four on each side
of a cardboard castle door. A crewcut,
trim announcer boomed across the crowd,
"Ladies and gentlemen, the Batavia Area
Bounding Retrievers' Homecoming Queen,
everybody's favorite Golden Girl, Miss
Clarissa Williams." And then she was
in the doorway, a bit piquant and a little
rebellious. She had a look that charmed
him, a touch Edwardian and softly romantic—
a belted coat worn with striped trousers

and a wide tie, a rose in her mouth.

He studied her; not one in three thousand
makes it in his world. Her body shape was
not in fashion. Her walk was angular,
imperfect, as if she'd be more comfortable
on all fours romping in a field.
But her cheekbones were perfect,
well defined, setting off her narrow nose
and stunning symmetrical jaw.

About him high school teachers, boys and girls,
their mothers and their fathers cheered.
All felt Miss Williams's energy. It was
very organic. She had charisma.

What is beauty, he thought, *but an ever
shifting shape, a fancy of the mind fitting
desires unknown and unacknowledged.*

He slipped backstage, the right man
in the right place. Though she did not come cheap,
he paid the price—he's rich, you know—
and shipped her east. The perfect cover girl,
she is, at once, the beauty and the beast.

Bat Boy Is Missing

He is not Robin, no good fellow
sidekick, puckish accomplice
of a comic book hero.

Nor is he lost, though his old-man
visage terrifies the breakfast
table from the milk carton side.

Almost bodiless (weightless to fly
though no membrane stretches from arm
to leg to form a fragile wing),
he is all head. His huge, round eyes
gaze blindly into light, bulge.
His cavernous mouth is open,
perhaps to scream, to make of his
gift of speech a curse. His ears flare
as large as a satellite dish
to catch the bounce of his cry
and locate him in himself apart
from brother, sister, friend.

We know him. He is a natural
child born of a mother's natural
love and a father's natural hope.
He is nothing more, nothing less
than a natural twist, a turn

of nature being nature.

But his mother winced,
and his father swore;
they named him Bat Boy—
and made him other.

Have you seen this child?

He is in the bedroom dark
crawling the heaving covers.

Meet the Amazing Half Man Half Pig

Each day he walks the thirty yards
back and forth between his house and barn.
You can see him, if you stop along
the road and lean casually against
his fence. His overalls and ballcap
show him up a farmer like every
other farmer in the valley.
But don't go close. He is a shy
one, easily spooked. He will not
be known. Watch him. You will see,
as he walks, the sudden lifting
of his very human hand to wipe
the round, flattened snout through which he
breathes the same barnyard air that
reaches you at the fence. You will see
the same hand scratching at the sharp
bristled ears grown high on his hoggy
head. You will never see him pick
and bite into a crisp, sweet apple.

He will not be known because he
cannot say himself, as he crosses
the worn path of his daily labor,
which pole is home. He wonders,
Am I the farmer or the farmed?
It matters more than you, staring

from the fence, can guess. You straddle
nothing deeper than convictions.

It troubles him, pouring milk
and slops into the trough, thinking
of ham and bacon, to see himself
looking up into his eyes. Will he
find his end as ignominious
as the one his snorting porcine
herd will find? Or will he be
laid out in glory, a necktie
bound about his weathered neck
and makeup plastered on his face,
the food chain broken, the body
torn only in the empty grave?

He knows himself as both and neither:
half man, half pig, half god and beast.
He longs, like you, to know himself:
a pig risen into manhood
or a man descending into pork,
like some wild god risking
everything to be his own creation.

Duck Hunters Shoot Angel

The thing was coming straight at me,
head high across the open water,
and it was big. I pulled up and let
loose with both barrels, dropping it
ten yards out. I turned to the dog
but it wouldn't retrieve,
just hung back in the blind whimpering.
It was twice her size anyway. Harold,
my partner, nearly blind himself
with keeping off the cold all morning,
just stared, muttering, "Holy shit, holy shit."
So I slogged out—breaking the ice,
sinking up to the waist, freezing
you know what—and dragged her back.

Big as she was, she weighed nothing.
I dumped her on Harold's feet.
He stood there, slack-jawed and dumb,
then he said, "Ya think it's in season?"
I lifted a wing, and damn, there underneath
it was an arm muscled like Hulk Hogan.
"I thought she was a big bird," I said,
mostly to myself, and dropped the wing,
but Harold had seen. "Sonabitch,"
he pointed, "You killed yourself
a male angel." "Shut up," I answered.

"Angels ain't neither male nor female.
Any fool knows that. What's more, ain't
no one can kill an angel, they're immortals."

"This one weren't," Harold said,
and he was right. It was dead.
Then the dog come alongside and begun
sniffing and then licking about it.
I pulled it away. It didn't seem right
even though the dog seemed somehow
to be affectionate-like and worshipful.

Harold realized the thing was flopped
on his feet, and he give it a little push,
getting aside from it, and it rolled over part
way coming to rest on those rough wings.
That's when I saw the face. It was
human-like and not very pretty, without
a beard, but awful to see. It scared me,
looking up like I was the one dead, like it
could see me and I wasn't making it happy.

"Ain't no angel," I said. I was thinking,
if it was an angel it woulda sung out
from the sky hosannas and not come in like
some buzz-bombing buzzard set on supper.

It woulda shouted, "Holy, Holy,"
and I woulda known to take off my shoes
'cause Christ himself was coming right
behind. But no, it just come on at me
like nothing you never seen, so I pulled
up and killed it. I was thinking that
when Harold gets to laughing. He just
plopped down in the cold muck,
clutched his big gut, and laughed.
"Oh," he gasped, grabbing for breath,
"You got Hell to pay." "You shut up,"
I said again. I coulda shot him
and buried him and the thing
and no one been the wiser,
but it was getting to look like an angel
to me. I couldn't think what else
it might be, so I left it with Harold
and the dog lying down looking
in its eyes, like it understood
something I didn't, and went and called
the sheriff. He come right along,
along with a Baptist preacher he rung up.

The preacher stood over the thing.
"That's an angel all right. Biggest one
I ever saw. Sure be a shame we won't

ever hear its word." And he looked
at me like I'd killed his God
and nailed up his church forever.

The sheriff said he couldn't see
I'd broken any laws. Angels ain't
protected or anything, but I don't know.
I ain't never killed no angel before
and ain't nothing no one can say
seem to be the right thing.

I Want to Have a
Space Alien's Baby

I didn't mind when she joined me
on my break at Starbucks. I'd met her
on the elevator coming and going
from an office on a floor near mine.
"I want to have a space alien's baby,"
she said. Froth from a caffe mocha
lined her lips like the milk mustache
of a little girl. I can't remember
what I said. If I said anything,
I don't think she heard, for she continued,
"I spent a night beyond the moon
one time. Aliens are wonderful lovers.
You know that old song about slow hands?
They have six of them." She stopped.
I looked aside, furtively checked my watch
preparing to mumble an excuse and flee
for the safety of my work, but something
held me. "Oh," she said. I could see
disappointment in her eyes. "You misunderstand.
It wasn't like you think, but don't ask me
to tell you more. I've hidden all that
in my heart. Talk cheapens things."

"I don't need to know," I said.
Then, without thinking, after sipping
my coffee, I added, "But there's something

other I should hear, isn't there?"

When she spoke again, her voice was changed,
softer, intense. "I was frightened," she said.
"A great light descended, enclosing me.
He was in it—such gentleness
I had never known. I yearned for him to stay.
And now he is risen from this world,
I yearn for him still. I want to give
myself again and have his child. I want
to birth tenderness for this world."

She looked long at me, said, "I'm called,"
and touched my hand. It recoiled.
Pushing back my chair, I burst out,
"Good God." At the word, she fled.

Merman Caught in
the South Pacific

We'd made landfall the night before,
and I'd run the dinghy in to find
the harbormaster and clear customs
for our stay. At the end of the dock
an American of massive girth
and large mouth was holding up a fish
about two feet long and telling
a crowd, cruisers and islanders,
"I won't say where I got him
or how, but he's not the first
I've caught. I might have been
trolling for tuna. I might have been
diving a reef. I'll only say
there's more where this one came from,
and I aim to harvest them for sale."

The power in his voice caught me,
and I stood still. The tail was all
of the fish I could see. It was
golden and deeply forked, protruding
from the speaker's clench. Without
seeing more, I knew the fish was one
I'd never seen. Then it thrust
upward in his hand. I should have
known nothing that color could be dead.
Its body was strong and narrow,

large scaled with green bars.
It twisted again and I saw more.
The scales turned to skin
the color of sunburn where the body
thickened into a tight stomach,
barrel chest, and muscular shoulders
and arms. A large fin, flared
like a marlin's, grew from its spine.
Its head, small with a face
screwed by pain, was human.
Clearly, it was breathing air.

Before the strangeness of the two,
the crowd was dumb, transfixed,
like fairgoers caught in a side
show spiel. Voiceless, the merman
clenched his fists at his waist.

Bizarre Creature Spotted
in Louisiana Bayou

He has no memory of birth.
He does not know if his mother
clawed away the steaming vegetation
of her nest when he began to squeal
and peck his fingernails against
a shell or if she cried at a sudden,
gripping pain and labored
through a night to push him
headlong into life.

He does not know if she took him
gently in her mouth, tossed him
into position in her teeth
and carried him to water
or if she held him to her breast
and gave him suck.

He does not remember the danger
of cruising fish or stalking heron
nor the darkness of a nursery night
and the retreating figure
of his only felt security.

He remembers only waking
to consciousness in mangrove waters,
in the bracken flux, half fresh

half salt, and knowing himself
by reflection full grown.

He saw, at once, a face
with sunken cheeks, skin pulled taut
about a grimace-smile, a chest
gaunt with ribs racked in line,
arms thin as flails ending
in hands given to touch and love,
and behind this his alligator half
stretched green and armored
where other human members
should have been.

Knowing himself both more and less
than we could bear, he eased
into the water and swam.
In the wilderness of his choosing,
he stopped and climbed onto a bank
where he has stayed unpartnered.

Some afternoons, when he is sure
of his hiddenness, he heaves himself
upright, a tripod, balanced on hind legs
and tail, and sings. Around him the birds
grow still, their silence an underscore
to the breaking joy of his risen hope.

Montana Police Shoot Bigfoot

Two innocents in the holy wild, the pair
stood gaping at the hairy heap of body
on the trail. What terrified them most, the boy
told us, was the silence of the pursuit.
In the bright afternoon, when she first saw
him digging roots across a flowered field
and they set off to intersect his course,
he was dumb. In the dimming light of dusk,
when he turned upon their looming curiosity,
he made no sound. And through the long dark,
as they wove among the trees, not even
an exhalation of his breath reached their ears.
A grunt or a low growl, they said, would have
buoyed their spirits, rallied them, and made him,
somehow, less than what he was, more human—
comprehensible. They knew him only
as *the other*, as something that did not
value them as they valued themselves.
We cannot know if what he did, he did
by choice, or if he simply stalked them like
a simple beast scenting simple prey.
Nor can we know, if choosing, he governed
what he did by some blunt morality
of kinship that reduced the pair to meat,
or if in anger or desire he trespassed bounds
and rose to sin. The hikers can tell us nothing
except how it seemed. Some consciousness,

they said, some grim intelligence, seemed
to herd them forward then stand off to watch
and wait, to observe before hounding them again.

He had no weapon. His body, a mossy boulder
with arms and legs rolling through the trees,
was weapon enough. Death, they knew, if it were
to come from him, would come as a brutal embrace
or a ripping of bone from bone. His presence,
overbearing, turned the holy wild to wilderness,
changed the innocents from pilgrims into refugees.

Through the night, they said, their only life
was language. No hurled stone or branch,
no threatening gesture slowed the beast.
Words, however, whether shouted at his shape
or spoken softly to each other, kept him off.
They babbled in the dark, found their camp, cell phone
and their GPS. While the dumb cold circled,
they called and called. At dawn, the troopers
arrived, the bullet, and the human wild.

Real Life Cat Woman Found in the Ozarks and She's Looking for Love

She's down and dirty in a lace bikini.
Where she found it is anybody's guess,
unless she tore it from a budding rival
walking, unsuspecting, hand in hand
with some dull partner in the woods.

Don't think on that. Consider this:
it does nothing flattering for her tail.
Though for the feline litheness of her thighs,
it does all a lusting voyeur could desire.
Her whiskers, dark and thick as a mustache,
twitch with eagerness. Her fingers, reaching out
to knead a lover, are clawed to tear.
Her lips curl back revealing saber teeth. No one
would call her smile becoming or say
how kittenish she looks. Nor would a gentleman
invite her long body to coil into a purring
pile of fur upon an unprotected lap.
She is danger daring the tame to play.

Think with what ferity she will meet her lover.

Think what fierce offspring might suckle safely
at her breast. Could any child nursed
on that wildness grow to find a place
in any world you want to know?

Think carefully. Some rank infusion—
In wildness is the preservation of the world—
might be the needed shot, the *Yes* humanity
has feared to speak to every other
calling from the brink. Are you the one?
Will you be her mate?

About John Leax

John Leax's books of poetry include *Reaching into Silence* (1974), *The Task of Adam* (1985), *Country Labors* (1991) and *Tabloid News* (2005). His novel, *Nightwatch,* was published in 1989. And his nonfiction works include *In Season and Out* (1985), *Standing Ground* (1991), *Out Walking* (2000) and *Grace Is Where I Live,* published originally in 1993 and reissued in a revised and expanded edition by WordFarm in 2004.

Leax gives several readings and lectures each year at various colleges, libraries and conferences. He has been featured as a panelist and seminar leader at Calvin College's biannual Festival of Faith and Writing. His articles, stories and poems have been widely published in anthologies and in periodicals such as *Books & Culture, The Chaffin Journal, Cold Mountain Review, Image, The Midwest Quarterly* and *River King Poetry Supplement.* He is a member of The Chrysostom Society, The Orion Society, The Association for the Study of Literature and the Environment, and the Nature Conservancy.

Also from WordFarm

Grace Is Where I Live:
The Landscape of Faith & Writing
John Leax

Grace Is Where I Live has inspired—even mentored—many writers, readers and teachers during the decade since it was first published. Here John Leax shares the experiences that shaped his life along with insights on choosing writing as a vocation, successful and failed teaching, identifying a personal "poetic," writing in different genres, writing from "placedness," and writing for a particular community. He wrestles with the "questions that must be asked" and ultimately offers "good news" about the struggles, trials and rewards of the writing life.

This new edition, marking the tenth anniversary of *Grace Is Where I Live,* includes the complete text of the original revised by Leax and expanded with a new preface, six recent essays, the poem "Vow" and a bibliography. Four different versions are available: print, ebook, audio book (abridged), and enhanced ebook (an ebook/audio book package).

Copies may be purchased from Amazon.com, from WordFarm at www.wordfarm.com, or by request at bookstores nationwide.

Colophon

The text of this book is set in Sabon, a revised version of Garamond designed by Jan Tschichold in the late 1960s. Classic, elegant and very legible, it is regarded as one of the most beautiful Garamond variations. Headlines and titles are set in Candida, designed by Jakob Erbar, released after his death in 1935, and revised throughout the next fifteen years. It has found common usage in magazines and newspapers as well as in larger sizes for signs and billboards.

Cover images are from Veer and iStockphoto. Cover filmwork, printing and binding is by Color House Graphics (Grand Rapids, Michigan).

The first edition is limited to one thousand five hundred copies. The first one hundred copies are signed and numbered.